HUMMINGBIRDS

GALLERY BOOKS
An Imprint of W. H. Smith Publishers Inc.
112 Madison Avenue
New York City 10016

This edition first published in U.S.
in 1991 by Gallery Books,
an imprint of W.H. Smith Publishers, Inc.
112 Madison Avenue, New York, New York 10016

ISBN 0-8317-9570-0

Printed and bound in Spain

For rights information about the photographs in
this book please contact:

The Image Bank
111 Fifth Avenue, New York, NY 10003

Producer: Solomon M. Skolnick
Writer: Scott Weidensaul
Design Concept: Lesley Ehlers
Designer: Ann-Louise Lipman
Editor: Joan E. Ratajack
Production: Valerie Zars
Photo Researcher: Edward Douglas
Assistant Photo Researcher: Robert V. Hale
Editorial Assistant: Carol Raguso

Title page: **Light as a feather, a hummingbird hovers at a bird-of-paradise flower,
sipping its nectar—the food that fuels the
hummer's dynamic metabolism.** *Opposite:*
**A male ruby-throated hummingbird drinks
from the blossoms of a wild columbine.
Many such "hummingbird flowers" are
colored red to catch the tiny bird's eye,
and bear their flowers away from their
leaves, which could catch the hummingbird's wings.**

When the subject is hummingbirds, super-latives come easily: brightest, smallest, fleetest. In fact, a hummingbird itself is a superlative, a minute, finely crafted creature no bigger (in most cases) than one's thumb, living life at a ferocious clip, agile beyond compare, with colors that border on garish artificiality. So small and fast are they that it is hard not to think of them as gorgeous insects.

Size notwithstanding, they are birds, merely modifications of the basic avian plan – two wings, a beak, two feet, and feathers. Some birds, using the same fundamentals, have developed webbed feet and waterproof feathers for swim-ming; others, like woodpeckers, are living drills, with padded skulls and chiseled beaks for splitting wood. In each case, form follows function. A hummingbird's function is to hover beside flowers and sip the nectar they contain. The evo-lutionary result is pure magic.

Hummingbirds are a strictly New World family, sprung from the tropical rain forests of South America but now spread across the Caribbean, Central America, and through North America as

Perched among the dead remnants of last year's meadow, a female ruby-throat is herself dulled by the pale sunshine, her iridescent feathers only giving a hint of their potential. The ruby-throat is the only species of hummingbird found in the East, making identification simple.

This page: **A male rufous hummingbird shifts position, and instantly his coppery gorget turns black—a dramatic example of how the light angle affects the colors of the hummingbird's iridescent feathers.** *Opposite:* **Although hummingbirds are, by and large, a tropical family, a few species have adapted to northerly climates. The rufous hummingbird, for instance, is found as far north as the Alaskan panhandle.**

Above: The calliope hummingbird (like this female) is the smallest bird in North America, just a fraction over three inches long. It is common in western meadows and well-watered canyons. *Opposite:* A baby calliope hummingbird opens wide for its lunch, a blend of nectar and tiny insects regurgitated by its mother. The nest, in the Tetons of Wyoming, is built of spider webs and lichens and is typical of hummingbirds.

far as southern Alaska and Canada. Most are small, although one Andean species is almost as big as a starling. The tiniest, the bee hummingbird (*Mellisuga helenae*) of Cuba, is two and one-quarter inches long, the smallest bird in the world, weighing less than seven-hundredths of an ounce. In all, more than 320 species are known. However, the figure cannot be precise, because new hummingbirds are still being discovered, particularly in the high cloud forests of the Andes.

For all their beauty, the most remarkable things about hummingbirds are hidden from view. Although a hummingbird's body is tiny, its surface area in comparison with other birds is much greater; therefore, it must metabolize energy at an insane pace in order to keep its body temperature at a constant level of about 103 degrees. They have pushed warm-blooded miniaturization to the limit; any further reduction in size from that of a tiny hummingbird would require more food than could be eaten.

A hummingbird can keep even with its body's demands during the day because it can feed whenever it must. But hummers don't fly at night, so they must conserve energy until the sun rises again. In the tropics, where nighttime temperatures

Although a male hummingbird's species is relatively easy to identify, females and immatures of many species cannot be separated in the field. This migrating immature, for instance, could be either an Allen's hummingbird or the closely related rufous.

This page: The tiny feet of these Allen's hummingbirds illustrate the commitment that hummers have made to life on the wing. A hummingbird's feet are so small that they cannot walk, only perch. If they need to move slightly on a branch, they must take off and land again. *Opposite:* Hummingbirds almost invariably lay two eggs, which in most species are no more than a half-inch long. The chicks grow rapidly, eventually stretching their tiny, pliable nest almost to the breaking point. This is a family of Anna's hummingbirds in California.

This page: Too fast even for a high-speed flash, the wings of a male Anna's hummingbird leave ghost images as he hovers at a flower to feed. A hummer's wings may beat as fast as 50 or 60 flaps per second, appearing only as a blur to the unaided eye.

This page: Probing deeply with his bill, an Anna's hummingbird sips nectar from a garden blossom, using his specially grooved tongue to channel the nectar into his throat. Most hummingbirds feed sporadically, interspersing trips to the flowers with short periods of rest.

This page: A female broad-tailed hummingbird tends her chicks in the Wyoming mountains, while at bottom, a newly hatched broad-tailed chick rests within its cushion of plant down and cobwebs. Females of this species often return each summer to the same nesting site, usually a horizontal tree branch that extends over a stream. *Opposite:* The broad-tailed hummingbird of the western mountains superficially resembles the male ruby-throated of the East, but the broad-tailed has a much longer and wider tail, as well as a crisper demarcation between the green and white of the undersides.

are fairly high, the hummingbird can simply perch quietly. However, energy conservation becomes a problem in mountains and deserts, where the temperature drops at night. To maintain a high metabolism in such cold conditions would actually call for an increase in food.

Many hummingbirds have adapted by borrowing a trick from mammals. They go into a torpor, similar to hibernation, that lasts through the night. Measurements on blue-throated hummingbirds (*Lampornis clemenciae*), for instance, showed that at an air temperature in the 90's, the bird's heartbeat would range between 480 and 1,200 per minute; however, it drops to only 36 per minute at night when the air temperature is around 60 degrees. In many of the hummingbirds tested, body temperatures dropped into the 50's or 60's, roughly half of the level attained during the day.

To fuel the daytime internal fire, a hummingbird needs lots of food and oxygen. Research indicates that hummers use up to eight times the oxygen needed by larger songbirds; for this

Preceding page: **A male black-chinned hummingbird pauses for an instant above a coral bean plant in the Santa Rita Mountains of Arizona. Common across the West, the black-chinned's gorget has a dark purple border, but the light must be exactly right for the color to be visible.** *This page:* **These black-chinned hummingbirds demonstrate the figure-eight motion of the wings that allows a hummer to hang motionless in the air—something no other bird can do. Although a hummingbird's wing bones are fused for strength, its shoulder joint is exceptionally limber, allowing such movement.**

This page: The "mustache" of the male Costa's hummingbird makes this South-western species one of the easiest to identify. An inhabitant of the desert, a Costa's nests in low shrubs and yucca, sometimes far from the nearest open water. *Opposite:* Like virtually all hummingbirds, the Costa's hummer is promiscuous; the male courts passing females by zooming through a huge U-shaped arc, whistling like a bullet. Once they have mated, the pair separates and the female handles all chick-rearing duties.

reason, their air passages and lungs are proportionately bigger. A hummingbird's heart is out-sized, too. In a hummingbird, the heart makes up nearly two and one-half percent of the entire body mass.

The hummer's blood supply feeds the muscles of the chest, which may make up more than one-fourth of the bird's total mass. Unlike most birds, in which the power stroke is the downward flap, hummingbirds must be able to exert power on both the upward and downward strokes in order to hover and to fly backward. At more than 50 beats per second, such flight obviously puts tremendous demands on the bird's muscles.

Every hummingbird known feeds on flower nectar and tiny insects. Nectar is rich in carbo-hydrates and the insects are rich in protein, but the hummingbird must nevertheless eat almost incessantly to keep pace with the demands of its body. Studies with rufous hummingbirds (*Selasphorus rufus*) revealed that they feed in spurts, about 15 times per hour with short periods of restful perching in between, because each time they feed, they fill their crops, then retire while their stomachs begin to digest the meal. They can eat no faster than their stomachs can process the food.

The violet-crowned hummingbird is common through much of Mexico, but only enters the U.S. in southeastern Arizona and the boot heel of New Mexico, where it inhabits the banks of wood-lined streams.

To reach the nectar, which is stored at the base of the flower's tubular corolla, most hummingbirds have evolved long, thin bills that can probe far into the blossom. The bill itself, however, plays no great role in the act of sipping; it merely serves as a sheath for the hummingbird's remarkable tongue, which is dipped into the nectar reservoir, withdrawn into the bill, then forced out again through the slightly open beak. The outward pressure brings the nectar in from the grooved tongue and it is swallowed as the hummer laps up another load.

There is little variation among hummingbird bills. Most are roughly a third or a fourth of the bird's total length, straight or slightly down-curved. That is a broad generalization, however, and there are many exceptions. The most remarkable bill is that of the sword-billed hummingbird (*Ensifera ensifera*). It has a four-inch rapier beak as long as its body and tail combined, which allows it to feed on the tubed flowers of a number of tropical plants – species like the passion-flower, with a four-inch corolla that puts the nectar beyond the reach of other birds and insects.

It was once thought that each hummingbird's bill corresponded to the shape of a particular flower. That is now known to be false, although those species with longer beaks tend to feed from longer, deeper blossoms because the competition for these flowers is less fierce. The stripe-tailed hummingbird (*Eupherusa eximia*) of Central America has a small beak – leading one to believe that it feeds on small flowers with shallow corollas. However, it uses its sharp beak to drill holes at the base of deeper flowers, thus gaining access to nectar that would ordinarily be out of its reach. The purple-crowned fairy (*Heliothryx barroti*) of Central and South America does the same thing, as do several other short-billed species. That is fine for the birds, but often not good for the plants, which may rely on hummingbirds for pollination.

Evolutionary pressures have also greatly modified the hummingbird's wings. In most birds, forward flight is the only kind possible, but a hummingbird's wing development and flight are different. The hummingbird's humerus, radius, and ulna are quite short and are fused. The carpals and phalanges (which correspond to the fingers in humans) are long, taking up most of the wings, and the

Above: Large and – for a hummingbird – relatively slow-moving, the blue-throated hummingbird is another Southwestern specialty, found in the U.S. only in southern Arizona and New Mexico, and in the Big Bend region of Texas. *Left:* Only the male has the blue throat – the female's throat is gray.

shoulder girdle is unusually flexible, so the wing can move freely on both the horizontal and vertical planes.

Add to these skeletal changes the hummingbird's phenomenally powerful chest muscles. Hummingbirds have deep keels, or sternums, that allow the anchoring of muscles that are heavy for the size of the bird: in a ruby-throated hummingbird (*Archilochus colubris*), the flight muscles may make up more than 30 percent of the body weight.

As a result of its unique wing structure and heavy musculature, a hummingbird can flap its wings in ways that other birds cannot, allowing it to fly in ways that seem equally impossible. To hover, a hummingbird holds its body almost upright, then flaps horizontally in a shallow figure eight. As the wings swing back, they tilt almost flat, forcing air upward, then are brought upright for the forward stroke, which drives air down. The net effect is to keep the hummingbird suspended as though hanging from an invisible thread. In terms of the amount of muscular energy that is expended, hovering is very costly, requiring tremendous exertions, but it makes the hummingbird's life of nectar-sipping possible.

This page: **The camera freezes a male blue-throated hummingbird in the midst of a hummer's most strenuous activity—hovering. Even at rest, a blue-throated hummer's heart beats 480 times a minute; the rate soars to 1,200 beats per minute when flying.**

This page: The crimson beak of a male broad-billed hummingbird almost matches the flowers on which he feeds, while the female's beak (left) is much duller. The broad-billed, like so many other hummingbirds, barely count as U.S. residents, just crossing the border from Mexico. *Opposite:* Light dances across the plumage of a male broad-billed hummingbird, providing a cool counterpoint to the flaming blossoms of an ocotillo, one of the more important food plants for desert hummingbirds.

To fly backward – something that even scientists believed impossible until high-speed photography proved that it could be done – a hummingbird reaches back with its wings, scooping into the air like a swimmer doing the backstroke. At rest, a hummingbird can't fold its wings into a compact package, as can most birds. All it can do is lap the permanently extended wings back over its tail, out of the way. During waking hours, however, the wings are rarely out of use. A hummingbird is so streamlined for a life of flight that its feet are tiny and all but useless for walking, so even a small shift of position calls for a momentary takeoff and landing.

Each species has its own flapping pace, but a hummingbird's wingbeat is fairly constant, regardless of the type of flight in which it is engaged. Most hummers average about 50 to 58 beats per second, and some have been measured at 200 per second in courtship flight – an astounding number, although not surprising when the size of the wing is taken into consideration: the smaller the wing, the faster it can be flapped.

This page: A rufous-breasted hermit lands on her nest, which is suspended from a palm frond in the rain forest of French Guiana. The hermits are a large group of tropical hummingbirds, including the green hermit (left), found in tropical and subtropical forests from Central America to Peru.

Above: The nest of the rufous-breasted hermit, built at the tip of a drooping leaf, is typical of the hermit clan. While such a site may seem precarious, it provides protection from snakes, which are unable to navigate the flimsy route. *Below, left:* A long-tailed hermit, a common Neotropical species, feeds at a hibiscus flower. *Right:* The reddish hermit is a South American bird, found from the Andes to the Atlantic.

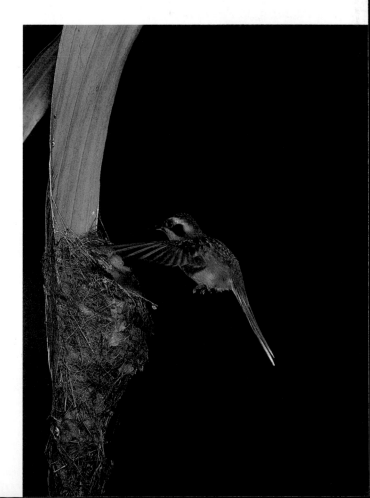

Small though they be, an average hummer's wings can move it along at a healthy clip. Ruby-throats in wind tunnels can make headway against winds up to 27 miles per hour (far less than the 60 miles per hour often cited for free-flying birds, probably achieved with the help of tail winds). Some tropical species have been timed in wind tunnels at much faster speeds, exceeding 45 miles per hour. Because of their small size and agility, hummingbirds usually seem to be moving faster than they actually are, as they swarm around a feeder or buzz overhead in a mountain meadow, those impossibly small wings a blur against the sky.

The hummingbird's small size and agility likewise make it difficult for predators to catch them. On those rare occasions when hummingbirds are caught, the predator is usually a falcon or an accipiter, the fastest and most agile of hawks. Others have been known to fall victim to large songbirds like orioles, to frogs, fish, and occasionally to tree-climbing snakes. Dragonflies and praying mantises sometimes catch hummingbirds instead of the insects they normally eat. The webs of large spiders, like the black-and-yellow argiope, sometimes ensnare hummers.

The white-chested emerald is a member of the large genus *Amazilia,* which contains some of the most exquisite of the tropical hummingbirds.

Preceding page: An Andean emerald opens its mouth and flicks out its tongue after feeding, a common behavior among hummingbirds. Andean emeralds are found in the subtropical zone of the Andes, from Ecuador to Peru. *This page, right:* A female blue-tailed emerald feeds one of her chicks, which, like all newly hatched hummingbirds, does not yet have a long, rapier-like beak. *Below:* A male glittering emerald does just that, throwing back sunlight in a dazzle of color that makes this South American species one of the most spectacular of hummingbirds.

Above: A tiny patch of colorless throat feathers gives the male white-chinned sapphire, perched on a branch in Colombia, his name. The hummer's scientific designation, *Hylocharis cyanus,* refers to the male's deep blue face. *Opposite:* Hummingbirds are found in a variety of habitats, from rain forests to mountain slopes far above the timberline. The rufous-chinned hummingbird is an inhabitant of scrublands throughout much of South America.

Just as hummingbirds are unique in their flying abilities, so too are they set apart by their riot of iridescent feathers. Much of the hummingbird's color is structural rather than pigmented, as in most other birds. The iridescent feathers of the hummingbird – usually at least those on the throat gorge and head of the males and on the back of both sexes – rely on layers of special cells that cover parts of the feathers. Light that hits these cells is broken apart. Some wavelengths are reinforced and intensified, while others are nullified through spectral interference. The resulting colors are amazingly vivid; unlike pigmented colors, however, they can be seen only when light hits the feathers at precisely the right angle. Thus, a hummingbird can shift its position slightly, and what had been a flaming gorget of red will suddenly quench and become dull.

Slight changes in feather structure, angle, and the distance between the interference cells can produce a kaleidoscope of colors, and it seems that hummingbirds as a group display almost every conceivable color. Reds, oranges, and golds are common, as are blues and violets. The most common iridescent color is green, found on the bodies and backs of many species; because the barbules of the back feathers are curved,

The sapphires are only a few of the more than 320 species of hummingbirds that inhabit the Western Hemisphere from southern Alaska to Tierra del Fuego at the extreme tip of South America.

Above: A hummingbird's sunbath becomes a feast for the eye as a male green violet-ear fluffs his feathers in the tropical sunlight. *Below, left:* The green violet-ear is occasionally found as far north as Texas, but the core of its range lies from Mexico to Bolivia. *Right:* The only touch of color on the brown violet-ear are the tufts of purple feathers that jut back over the bird's ear openings. *Opposite:* The sparkling violet-ear, a common hummingbird of scrublands and pastures in northern South America, is identified by its large size and dark chest patch, which the green violet-ear lacks.

A green violet-ear hovers at a coral bean plant. Green violet-ears are found in oak forests and along the edges of fields in the highlands extending south from central Mexico.

rather than flat as in the gorget, the color can be seen from almost every angle. But most of those colors can be found only on males, while the females get lost in the shuffle — which is the way nature intended it to be.

Female hummers tend (with some exceptions) to be much plainer than their mates, but that makes sense when one considers that the females do not need the bright courtship plumage the males use to attract mates. In fact, colors — even those of such a fickle nature as iridescence — would be a hazard as a female sits on her clutch of two white eggs through the two-and-one-half-week incubation, and the three and one-half more weeks before the chicks can fend for themselves. The female, who tends the nest alone, leaves it only for brief feeding periods.

Just as a mammal is not covered uniformly with fur, neither is a bird covered at random with feathers. In almost all birds

Above: The green-fronted lancebill lives up to its name, with a beak nearly as long as its body, although another South American hummer, the sword-billed hummingbird, has an even longer beak. *Left:* A green-crowned brilliant rests quietly in the rain forest of Monteverde, Costa Rica. *Opposite:* In the cloud forests of the Costa Rican highlands, where fog produces exceptionally lush rain forests, a female mountain-gem rests between feeding trips.

Preceding page: A green-backed fire-crown feeds on the dangling blossoms of a hummingbird flower, which obligingly hangs its corollas away from interfering foliage. The fire-crown is found farther south than any other hummingbird, in the bleakness of Patagonia, as well as the Juan Fernandez Islands 400 miles off the Chilean coast. *Below:* One of the classiest hummingbirds is the white-necked jacobin of Central America.

they grow in tracts, sprouting in neatly ordered rows, then blossoming up and out to shingle the bird completely. It will come as no surprise that hummingbirds have the fewest feathers on a per-bird basis – about 1,000 for a ruby-throated hummingbird, compared with more than 25,000 for a tundra swan. But that figure is misleading. For its size, the hummingbird has far more feathers than larger birds have; a hummingbird has only one-tenth the skin area of a brown thrasher, but it has one-half the number of feathers.

Birds make poor fossils, so we can only guess what the hummingbird's ancestors looked like. However, it is reasonable to suppose that the ancestral hummingbird was lured to flowers first by the insects that the flowers attracted. However, after discovering the rich store of food that nectar represents, those individuals with somewhat longer bills and tongues prospered, and passed those traits on to their offspring.

As hummingbirds have adapted to flowers, so, too, have some flowers adapted to hum-

This page, top to bottom: **The copper-rumped hummingbird of Venezuela is, like many hummers, aggressive in defending a feeding territory, chasing away other hummingbirds and even large, nectar-feeding insects. The female black-throated mango has a distinctive black stripe down her undersides; her mate's breast is pure black. The minute size of a hummingbird's feet are clearly shown in this photograph.** *Opposite:* **Bizarre quills mark the racquet-tailed hummingbird of South America, also known as the "puff-leg" because of the fluffy down feathers that billow out around its legs. Racquet-tailed hummingbirds are native to the foothills of the Andes.**

Just over three inches long, the male
violet-bellied hummingbird is a jewel in
feathers. It lives in the tropical forests of
Central America and the northern edge of
South America. *Following pages, left:*
Every barbule on every feather glistens on
this Brazilian bronze hummingbird. The
structural difference between the pigmented breast feathers and the iridescent
feathers of the head and back is easy to
see. *Right:* The white-tipped sicklebill's
sharply curved beak is designed to let the
hummingbird feed on the deep flowers of
tropical heliconias; unlike many hummers,
the relatively heavy sicklebill perches
while feeding, rather than hovering.

mingbirds. In North America, hummingbirds join with insects to pollinate many species of wildflowers, but in the tropics quite a few flowering plants have evolved to cater solely to hummers.

When the hummingbird sidles up for a drink and slips its bill into the flower, it will likely brush against the anthers, which deposit pollen on its bill or head. In fact, on many hummingbird flowers the anthers curve out and up from the front of the plant to facilitate this interaction. When the bird visits the next flower, the tiny pollen grains are rubbed off on the plant's stigma, effecting fertilization.

Hummingbirds are a family still wedded to the tropics. The closer one gets to the equator, the greater the variety of hummingbird species; as many as a third of them live within five degrees of it. Despite this abundance of forms, each hummingbird is adapted to a slightly different ecological niche, to avoid direct competition with its relatives. Many species may inhabit the same forest but feed at different levels, or on different flowers. Although hummingbirds as a group are most successful in the tropics, they have shown adaptability to a wide range of habitats, from moist jungle clearings to cold mountain slopes.

This page: Not all hummingbirds are minute – the giant hummingbird of South America is the Goliath of the family, at eight and a half inches long. While its length is nearly that of a thrush, the giant hummer is much more lightly built than a songbird.

Flower mites congregate around the nostrils of a long-tailed hermit, as they hitch a ride from blossom to blossom. Hummingbirds provide a convenient transportation system for the tiny arthropods, which do not harm the bird during their brief stay.

The flowers of a fuchsia lure a Brazilian woodnymph. Hummingbirds, with their gorgeous colors, have inspired a host of descriptive names—starthroats, sunbeams, mountain-gems, azurecrowns, sunangels and hillstars, just to name a few.

In North America the rufous hummingbird and the ruby-throat are the northernmost representatives of the group, while in South America the green-backed firecrown (*Sephanoides sephanoides*) has adapted to similarly harsh conditions in Tierra del Fuego at the extreme southern end of the continent. A subspecies of the firecrown, the Juan Fernandez hummingbird (*Sephanoides fernandensis*) occupies the Juan Fernandez Archipelago some 400 miles west of the Chilean coast. But wider expanses of ocean have defeated the hummingbird, which cannot cross the Atlantic or Pacific oceans. Consequently, no hummingbirds occupy the tropical and semitropical forests of Asia and Africa, even though environmental conditions there would be perfect for them.

That is not to say it will never happen; rufous hummingbirds have demonstrated an adaptability to cold and, conceivably, if they continue to spread north along the Alaskan coast, they might make the short jump across the icy Bering Strait to Asia, where a whole new world awaits their breathtaking beauty.

Above: A male red-tailed comet does an end-run around a large flower, slipping his bill in the back – getting the nectar, but avoiding the pollen-bearing anthers that protrude from the front. Hummingbirds often probe the nooks and crannies of flowers looking for tiny insects and spiders. *Opposite:* A red-tailed comet displays the rigid, elongated wings of the hummingbird family, which allow such masterful control of the air.

Beneath a bower of red foliage, a female ruby-topaz hummingbird patiently incubates her eggs, preparing to raise yet another generation of feathered royalty.

Index of Photography

Page Number	Photographer	Page Number	Photographer
Title Page	Stephen Dalton/NHPA	37	P. Morris/ARDEA London Ltd.
3	Wayne Lankinen	38-39	M. D. England/
4-5	Mike Price/Survival Anglia		ARDEA London Ltd.
6 (2)	Tim Fitzharris	40 Top	Kenneth W. Fink/
7	Tim Fitzharris		ARDEA London Ltd.
8	Anthony Mercieca	40 Bottom Left	Stephen Dalton/NHPA
9	Jeff Foott	40 Bottom Right	Kenneth W. Fink/
10-11	C. Allan Morgan		ARDEA London Ltd.
12 (2)	Betty Randall	41	Dennis Avon/
13	François Gohier		ARDEA London Ltd.
14 (2)	François Gohier	42-43	Stephen Dalton/NHPA
15 (2)	François Gohier	44 Top	Anthony Mercieca/
16 (3)	Jeff Foott		Photo Researchers, Inc.
17	G. C. Kelley	44 Bottom	C. Allan Morgan
18	G. C. Kelley	45	Gerard Lemmo
19 (3)	Betty Randall	46	François Gohier
20 Top	François Gohier	47	Kenneth W. Fink/
20 Bottom	C. Allan Morgan		ARDEA London Ltd.
21	C. Allan Morgan	48 Top & Center	M. D. England/
22-23	C. Allan Morgan		ARDEA London Ltd.
24 Top	Anthony Mercieca	48 Bottom	Anthony Mercieca
24 Bottom	G. C. Kelley	49	John S. Dunning/
25	G. C. Kelley		Photo Researchers, Inc.
26 Top	G. C. Kelley	50-51	John S. Dunning/
26 Bottom	C. Allan Morgan		ARDEA London Ltd.
27 (3)	G. C. Kelley	52	Anthony Mercieca
28 (2)	Betty Randall	53	John S. Dunning/
29	G. C. Kelley		Photo Researchers, Inc.
30 Top	Jany Sauvanet/	54 Top	Anthony Mercieca/
	Photo Researchers, Inc.		Photo Researchers, Inc.
30 Bottom	M. D. England/	54 Bottom	Kenneth W. Fink/
	ARDEA London Ltd.		Photo Researchers, Inc.
31 Top	M. D. England/	55	Adrian Warren/
	ARDEA London Ltd.		ARDEA London Ltd.
31 Bottom Left	Jany Sauvanet/	56-57	Anthony Mercieca
	Photo Researchers, Inc.	58 Top	Anthony Mercieca/
31 Bottom Right	Jany Sauvanet/NHPA		Photo Researchers, Inc.
32-33	M. D. England/	58 Bottom	Anthony Mercieca
	ARDEA London Ltd.	59	Edward R. Degginger/
34	Dennis Avon/		Bruce Coleman Inc.
	ARDEA London Ltd.	60	François Gohier
35 Top	F. Köster/Survival Anglia	61	Kenneth W. Fink/
35 Bottom	Haroldo Palo Jr./NHPA		Photo Researchers, Inc.
36	John S. Dunning/	62-63	M. D. England/
	ARDEA London Ltd.		ARDEA London Ltd.